T0077916

**TYRONE A. PERREIRA, Ph.D, MEd**

GRAD SCHOOL 101

**BALBOA.**PRESS

A DIVISION OF HAY HOUSE

Balboa Press books may be ordered through booksellers or by contacting:

Balboa Press
A Division of Hay House
1663 Liberty Drive
Bloomington, IN 47403
www.balboapress.com
844-682-1282

Because of the dynamic nature of the Internet, any web addresses or links contained in this book may have changed since publication and may no longer be valid. The views expressed in this work are solely those of the author and do not necessarily reflect the views of the publisher, and the publisher hereby disclaims any responsibility for them.

The author of this book does not dispense medical advice or prescribe the use of any technique as a form of treatment for physical, emotional, or medical problems without the advice of a physician, either directly or indirectly. The intent of the author is only to offer information of a general nature to help you in your quest for emotional and spiritual well-being. In the event you use any of the information in this book for yourself, which is your constitutional right, the author and the publisher assume no responsibility for your actions.

Any people depicted in stock imagery provided by Getty Images are models, and such images are being used for illustrative purposes only. Certain stock imagery © Getty Images.

Print information available on the last page.

ISBN: 978-1-9822-7158-9 (sc)
ISBN: 978-1-9822-7159-6 (e)

Balboa Press rev. date: 07/27/2021

*To Travis — Thank you for shining bright during my darkest hours.*

*The world can be harsh. The least we can do is be kind to ourselves, those we love, and those whose paths we cross.*

# ACKNOWLEDGEMENTS

*A special thank you to all who helped and inspired me along the way.*

Jan Barnsley
Whitney Berta
Adalsteinn Brown
Lynn & Roger Christie
Rhonda C. Cockerill
Liane Ginsburg
Monique Herbert
Audrey Laporte
Milree Latimer
Anita Morehouse
Laurie Morrison
Desmond & Yvonne Perreira
Milo & Bella Perreira
Romain Perreira & Jon Rowan
Sean Perreira & Paul Dewsbury
Laure Perrier
Christine Shea
Tina Smith
Sharon E. Straus
Mary-Louise Vanderlee
Travis S. Wingate

# Contents

# PREFACE

So why did you decide to go to graduate school? Every time someone asks me this question, they laugh at my response, "Just for fun." However, I ended up getting more out of my degree than I could have ever imagined. One primary reason for this was that I aligned myself with caring faculty that put my needs ahead of their own. We have all heard horror stories about student–supervisor experiences. One friend I recall saying, 'I would never wish grad school on my worst enemy.' But, it does not have to be this way.

The content within this book is based on my personal experience, basic project management skills, and great advice from other students and colleagues. This book is not intended to be a long, arduous read. Instead, the objective is to briefly highlight critical conversations to have, essential points to remember, and helpful tips to get you that degree. Short exercises are inserted throughout to help you organize, plan and manage your graduate work. Trust me, although the activities will only take a few minutes, they will help to keep you focused. This book also acts as a sort of passport for you. Instead of a stamp documenting every country you have been to, this book documents your journey from start to finish, from program admission to convocation. Depending on your degree, it will help you and your supervisor, if you have one, fill out your annual progress reports and document key decisions. It will help you to track your meetings, action items, and completed tasks.

Some professional graduate programs do not require a supervisor or the completion of a thesis. As such, there are a few sections in this book that you may be tempted to skip. Even though these chapters may not apply to you and your program, they do contain helpful hints that you may be able to pass on to others.

Now, let the fun begin.

# GET THE FACTS

When I completed my Master of Education, I remember struggling to decide whether or not I wanted to do a thesis or project. My wonderful supervisor, Dr. Mary-Louise Vanderlee, pointed out that both were an equal amount of work. As I understood it at the time, the main difference was whether or not I wanted to do a final oral defence or simply hand in a final paper. I opted to hand in a final paper. If there is even the slightest possibility that you may eventually complete a doctorate, take a look at the admission requirements of potential programs that you may be interested in. When I first decided to apply for my doctorate, the online admission requirements clearly stated that I must have a 'thesis master's degree.' I interpreted that to mean I would not be accepted as I did not complete an oral defence. Well, I was devastated and remember thinking, there is no way in hell I am doing another master's. So, I decided to reach out directly to the program director. Well, lo and behold, I received detailed information on what to include and emphasize in my letter of intent. Don't give up.

Admission requirements are relatively straightforward. However, if you do not meet all of the criteria exactly, do not give up. Contact the graduate department directly, especially if you are a mature student with a great deal of experience in your field. Do not simply rely on what is posted on websites. If I did that, I would not have applied to my graduate program. Remember, universities must set a standard and have basic requirements. However, this does not rule you out. Sell yourself.

**The same goes for funding.** Programs often have scholarships and student funding available. Look into it! This is going to be a recurring theme throughout this book. You are responsible for your education and completing it. You have to make everything happen. Many incredible people will help you along the way, but it is up to you at the end of the day.

# SUPERVISOR SELECTION

**Catch 22.** Recognize the potential pros and cons of selecting a very well-accomplished supervisor. Yes, it looks great on your CV, and you can learn a lot. However, remember that these individuals will likely have busy schedules, travel frequently, and be overextended. You will need to be patient, communicate clearly, and be direct about your needs. Not only may it be difficult to book meetings, but they may require more time to review documents and provide feedback. Having said that, they may still be a phenomenal mentor. Just acknowledge that this may be a reality and know what you are signing up for. If you are lucky, like I was, your supervisor may use their time at the airport to read your work or even review it while on vacation. Thank you, Dr. Whitney Berta.

**Interview them.** Some supervisors do not work through the summer. As funny as that may sound, they are human too, have families, and need time off. Just have these discussions in advance. Another vital conversation is whether your supervisor plans on taking a sabbatical. This is not necessarily a 'red flag'; it may simply limit your contact or communication in some cases. But, again, you need to have these conversations. An additional critical question to ask is whether you are free to select a topic or are required to work on one of your supervisor's projects.

**Interview other students.** Speak to other students who have been supervised by your person of interest. Especially former students. They will tell it like it is. Students currently being supervised may feel obliged to say good things since they have a lot at stake.

**The perfect supervisor.** In my opinion, a supervisor is there to help guide and mentor you. They should help you determine what you are genuinely interested in and help you to refine your research question. They want you to succeed and take pride in your accomplishments.

**The dark side.** I have heard and witnessed many horrible stories about supervisors. Thank goodness I did not personally experience this. Your supervisor should never put you down or make you feel incompetent. You are in graduate school, and incompetence did not get you there. Do not get me wrong; they will, and should, challenge you and provide a great deal of constructive feedback. However, no one, and I mean NO ONE, has the right to demean you. If this is occurring, you need to switch supervisors. I assure you; you do not want to spend years working closely with someone that treats you poorly. If your supervisor is causing you a great deal of stress rather than calming you down, then something is wrong. Finally, be wary of supervisors who tend to be first authors on student work. Supervisory status does not equate with authorship. Remember, this is your time to shine. If you do the work, you get the credit.

# BE KIND TO YOURSELF AND YOUR LOVED ONES

One of the best pieces of advice I ever received in life was to be kind to myself; thank you, Dr. Sharon Straus. This extends far beyond graduate school. Take time for yourself, family and friends. The one mantra I always use is "Family first, school, then work." Of course, you can disagree regarding the second and third options. Still, there is no question regarding the first, and don't let anyone ever tell you differently.

My partner used to joke, "That degree is half mine!" There is some truth to this. I am not a marriage counsellor, but what I will say is this, spoil your partner. It is way too easy to become so absorbed in your work that you neglect your spouse, friends, and family. Oh, and if you have pets, don't forget them either. My partner, Travis Wingate, and my two puppies Milo and Bella, got me through the hard times.

**Life gets in the way.** Sometimes unfortunate personal circumstances arise. Relationship problems, illness, death of a close friend or family member. I have heard about it all and, unfortunately, experienced it all as well. What I will say is this. Take the time you need. You will be far more productive, taking time off. Some believe it is better to throw yourself into your work; dive right into the deep end. You do

5

what is best for you. Talk about it. Talk, talk, talk. If it is a death, allow yourself time to grieve. Then, when the time is right, focus only on the positive and remember the good times. I know, I know, that's an entirely different book. Back to graduate school.

**Health and wellness.** Let's face it, this experience at some point or another is going to be stressful. It is amazing what a short break and/or even going away on vacation can do for you. It is easy to get caught up in your work and want to keep plowing through. Avoid sensory overload. Think about how much time you spend processing information, listening to music, watching TV, surfing the web, writing, reading, etc. The list goes on and on.

I won't preach. Ensure you eat well, sleep well, exercise, and socialize. You will be spending an enormous amount of time studying. Even if you do not practice meditation, take the time to do absolutely nothing.

# BUDDY UP

If possible, ask your supervisor if anyone slightly ahead of you in the program might be willing to meet with you and act as a mentor. This can prove to be very beneficial. You can learn from their mistakes, ask questions, and even share experiences. No, we are not talking about 'rainbows and unicorns,' but it is incredible how much you learn from someone who has 'learned the hard way,' so to speak. They can share their 'what not to do' with you, their views on professors and courses, remind you to fill out forms, and even help calm your nerves by sharing their experiences. Consider this a 'pay-it-forward act.' Hopefully, you will do the same for new students joining the program. Many mentors and mentees I know have become good friends over the years. Shout out to Dr. Laure Perrier, mentor extraordinaire.

# COURSE SELECTION

Regardless of your degree, you will have mandatory courses and hopefully a few elective ones. Often it is not a bad idea to get your required courses over with as soon as you can. Pay close attention to when courses are offered. There is nothing worse than realizing the one class you need, or plan to take, is not available at a time convenient for you. Go figure, right!

**Required courses.** Required courses, sometimes called mandatory or core courses, refer to courses that all students in a particular program must complete. Once again, get the facts. If you have taken a similar course elsewhere, see if you are eligible for transfer credit. If you don't ask, you won't receive.

**Electives.** Many programs allow for elective courses. Some programs provide a list of options for you to choose from, but you can often select a class external to your department. Let's be realistic. Some folks search for 'bird courses' to fulfill elective requirements. For those unfamiliar with this term, it refers to courses known to be 'easy.' Do yourself a favour and take a class that will help further your knowledge and expertise in what you are studying. This can put you miles ahead of your colleagues, not that I recommend comparing your progress to others. Comparing to others is a dangerous mistake. Focus on you.

**Consider reading courses and internships.** I did not know these were even options. Each university may be different. Reading courses and internships often require program director approval. They likely need a certain number of hours of work and graded assignments. I was fortunate to have the opportunity to complete an online course from another institution in systematic reviews and meta-analysis. I was able to complete it at my own pace. Although I won't go into detail, I had to submit the course syllabus, complete quizzes, hand in assignments, and then request a final grade from the professor. Speak with your supervisor and department to determine if a reading course or internship is possible.

# TASK 1

*Complete **Table 1.** Record each course you plan on taking, whether it is required, and when it is offered. Modify as necessary.*

**Table 1. Courses**

|  | Course ID | Course Title | Course Type<br>R = Required<br>E = Elective | Date |
|---|---|---|---|---|
| 1. |  |  |  |  |
| 2. |  |  |  |  |
| 3. |  |  |  |  |
| 4. |  |  |  |  |
| 5. |  |  |  |  |
| 6. |  |  |  |  |
| 7. |  |  |  |  |
| 8. |  |  |  |  |
| 9. |  |  |  |  |
| 10. |  |  |  |  |

# TASK 2

*Complete **Table 2**. This will help you, your supervisor, and committee members manage expectations. Modify as necessary.*

## Table 2. Course Plan Template

| COURSE NAME | YEAR ONE | | | | | | | | | | | | YEAR TWO | | | | | | | | | | | | YEAR THREE | | | | | | | | | | | | YEAR FOUR | | | | | | | | | | | |
|---|---|---|---|---|---|---|---|---|---|---|---|---|---|---|---|---|---|---|---|---|---|---|---|---|---|---|---|---|---|---|---|---|---|---|---|---|---|---|---|---|---|---|---|---|---|---|---|---|
| | SEPT | OCT | NOV | DEC | JAN | FEB | MAR | APR | MAY | JUN | JUL | AUG | SEPT | OCT | NOV | DEC | JAN | FEB | MAR | APR | MAY | JUN | JUL | AUG | SEPT | OCT | NOV | DEC | JAN | FEB | MAR | APR | MAY | JUN | JUL | AUG | SEPT | OCT | NOV | DEC | JAN | FEB | MAR | APR | MAY | JUN | JUL | AUG |
| Sample Course A | | | | | | | | | | | | | | | | | | | | | | | | | | | | | | | | | | | | | | | | | | | | | | | | |
| Sample Course B | | | | | | | | | | | | | | | | | | | | | | | | | | | | | | | | | | | | | | | | | | | | | | | | |
| Course 1 | | | | | | | | | | | | | | | | | | | | | | | | | | | | | | | | | | | | | | | | | | | | | | | | |
| Course 2 | | | | | | | | | | | | | | | | | | | | | | | | | | | | | | | | | | | | | | | | | | | | | | | | |
| Course 3 | | | | | | | | | | | | | | | | | | | | | | | | | | | | | | | | | | | | | | | | | | | | | | | | |
| Course 4 | | | | | | | | | | | | | | | | | | | | | | | | | | | | | | | | | | | | | | | | | | | | | | | | |
| Course 5 | | | | | | | | | | | | | | | | | | | | | | | | | | | | | | | | | | | | | | | | | | | | | | | | |
| Course 6 | | | | | | | | | | | | | | | | | | | | | | | | | | | | | | | | | | | | | | | | | | | | | | | | |
| Course 7 | | | | | | | | | | | | | | | | | | | | | | | | | | | | | | | | | | | | | | | | | | | | | | | | |
| Course 8 | | | | | | | | | | | | | | | | | | | | | | | | | | | | | | | | | | | | | | | | | | | | | | | | |
| Course 9 | | | | | | | | | | | | | | | | | | | | | | | | | | | | | | | | | | | | | | | | | | | | | | | | |
| Course 10 | | | | | | | | | | | | | | | | | | | | | | | | | | | | | | | | | | | | | | | | | | | | | | | | |

# DECIDING ON A THESIS TOPIC

My best advice to you is to select a topic that you are interested in and passionate about. You will be spending long hours reading, writing, and often boring your friends with stories about your research – I am joking, sort of. Ideas will come to you at the most random times. Figure out the best way to keep track of them. I have included a spot at the end of this book for you. See Appendix One.

Your supervisor may have many ideas as well, and even a few projects on the go. Sounds great, right? Right? Let me share my nightmare with you. I changed my topic four times. If you are wondering, yes, I also changed supervisors each time as well. My first area of interest was post-cardiac arrest hypothermia. My second was community paramedicine. My third was knowledge translation and data visualization. Each time, something just did not sit right with me. The topics did not feel like my projects. They did not excite me. Pay close attention to how you feel when selecting your topic. When you engage a potential supervisor to speak about possible research questions, be aware of how you feel. It is easy to get caught up and influenced by an enthusiastic, charismatic investigator who loves what they do. After starting my program, I realized that I was trying to select research questions that were more interesting to my supervisor than me.

So, you must be wondering, how did I finally settle on a research area of interest? Dr. Whitney Berta, who later became my supervisor, kindly asked me, "What are you interested in?" Just like that, I was speechless. For those who know me, that is rare. I could not come up with an answer. I had to go away and think about it. Whatever your subject area, make sure that you are interested and excited about your topic. You will be doing this for the next few years and, hopefully, continue in your field afterwards. If you are wondering what I settled on, not to worry, I discuss this shortly.

This is a time to be selfish. Graduate work is about you. You are dedicating a lot of your time to this work. Make sure you are passionate about it. There is absolutely no point in being miserable. If you do not enjoy your work, you likely will not be motivated to complete it.

# TASK 3

*Complete **Table 3.** What interests you? Although you may not be able to fill this in thoroughly, list your top areas of interest and speak with your supervisor about them.*

**Table 3. Topics of Interest**

| |
|---|
| 1. |
| 2. |
| 3. |
| 4. |
| 5. |

# ASSIGNMENTS

Try your best to always keep the big picture in mind and think about being efficient. In addition to gaining content knowledge in each course, think about how you can incorporate each assignment into your final thesis or project. Have a conversation about this with your professors and brainstorm. As common sense as this may sound, you would be surprised at how often this is not done.

**Think publications!** Talk to your professors about potential journals that might be interested in your work. Check the journal website for the aim, scope, and readership. If you are still unsure, contact the editor with an abstract or summary of your manuscript and ask if they might be interested. Speak with your professors and see if you can format your papers according to potential journal formatting guidelines. This can save you hours of work later. Reviewing articles from peer-reviewed journals in your field can help you when constructing your manuscripts. Publishing as you go not only helps build your CV but can also give you a bit more ground to stand on during your proposal or final defence. Imagine being able to say to an examiner that your work has been peer-reviewed and published. BOOM! Mic drop.

# TASK 4

*Complete **Table 4.** You likely will not be able to complete the entire table right away. However, speak with your professors. You may be able to determine which assignments may contribute to your thesis or project (e.g., developing a conceptual framework, a scoping review, or a proposal). You can also tentatively list what you hope to gain from each course so that when your professor asks you on the first day what your objective is for the class, you will look like a superstar.*

**Table 4. Course Objective & Take Away**

|  | Course | Objective & Take Away |
|---|---|---|
| 1. | | |
| 2. | | |
| 3. | | |
| 4. | | |
| 5. | | |
| 6. | | |
| 7. | | |
| 8. | | |
| 9. | | |
| 10. | | |

# TASK 5

*Complete **Table 5**. Once again, you may not complete this right away, but it is great to start thinking about your potential publications. In addition, you can use this to brainstorm with both your supervisor and your committee members.*

**Table 5. Potential Publications**

|   | Topic | Potential Journal |
|---|-------|-------------------|
| 1. |       |                   |
| 2. |       |                   |
| 3. |       |                   |
| 4. |       |                   |
| 5. |       |                   |

# COMMITTEE SELECTION

Much of what was written in the section regarding supervisor selection applies here as well. Screen potential committee members. Ask your supervisor for suggestions. Speak with students who have had these individuals on their committees.

You have to think about their schedule and ability to provide timely feedback. I cannot emphasize this enough. Don't think of this as an uncomfortable conversation. You want to be upfront and discuss both their expectations and yours. Remember, this is a collaborative venture. Leave any attitude at home. These folks are there for you.

# TASK 6

*Complete **Table 6**. Brainstorm and speak to others about potential committee members.*

**Table 6. Potential Committee Members**

|    | Name, Location |
|----|----------------|
| 1. |                |
| 2. |                |
| 3. |                |
| 4. |                |

# THE 30,000-FOOT VIEW

As soon as people find out you are doing graduate work, be prepared to tell them what you are studying. If you are conducting research, be prepared to tell them what knowledge gap you are filling. What is unique about your work? What are your contributions and the implications of your research?

Now develop a sound bite; in other words, summarize your thesis in one short sentence. You will be asked time and time again about your work. In social settings by family and friends, in class, at work, at your proposal and defence. You will even be asked after you graduate, not only in job interviews but also anytime someone finds out your credentials. So, save yourself many long, lost, confused blank stares, and come up with a concise way of stating, 'This is what I study.'

Let's use my thesis topic, for example. For those genuinely interested, I might say:

> *My research is based on extant research in organization science and organizational psychology. I used a multivariate analysis technique of structural equation modelling to develop and test a framework that I created. This framework includes an array of work attitudes (e.g., organizational commitment,*

*perceived support, and perceptions of justice) shown in disparate studies to have independent effects on work motivation, workplace behaviours, and work performance. One outcome of particular interest is extra role behaviours, which are often referred to as organizational citizenship behaviours. The results afford original and highly significant insights into the inter-relationships amongst the constructs of work context, work attitudes, workplace behaviours, and work performance.*

Crystal clear, right? Instead of going into this long-winded summary, I could also state:

*I look at how one's work environment influences their work attitudes, which impacts their behaviour.*

For those just being polite, I might say:

*I study work motivation and performance.*

The last is usually the quickest, then it allows others to ask questions if interested. Often in social settings, they won't!

## TASK 7

Your turn. Regardless of what stage you are at, create a short, one-sentence soundbite describing your research or area of interest. Come up with a few different versions. Refine them over time.

1. _____
   _____
   _____

2. _____
   _____
   _____

3. _____
   _____
   _____

# TAKE CHARGE - SCHEDULE MEETINGS WELL IN ADVANCE

You must take charge and manage your graduate work. Yes, your supervisor and committee are senior to you; however, you need to make things as easy for them as possible. These are busy people. You are ultimately responsible for staying on top of your work. Therefore, you need to keep things moving. One of the best ways I have found to do this is to schedule regular meetings. Don't wait for your supervisor to approach you. Take charge and make it happen.

Get in the habit of making all of your meetings professional. You do not have to go overboard, but at least be organized. Use a template with clear agenda items. See **Appendix Two – Meeting Template.** This is your dedicated time to ask questions. Start with action items agreed up from your previous meeting. Provide status updates. Before you end your session, agree on action items and due dates. Also, if you do not have regularly scheduled meetings, which I highly recommend, book your next meeting. If you have regularly scheduled meetings, then confirm your next one.

**One-on-one meetings with your supervisor.** You must meet regularly with your supervisor. This can help ensure you:

- Are on the right track

- Both are on the same page concerning your progress and timelines
- Have dedicated time to ask questions or get signatures when needed (i.e., for ethics applications, reference letters, etc.)
- Follow-up on any outstanding items

**Meeting with committee members.** The frequency of meetings is entirely up to you and your committee. If you are struggling to get your committee members together for a meeting, speak to your supervisor. Many of them have a way of 'moving mountains,' so to speak. So again, you need to take charge.

*Communicate, communicate, oh and did I mention, communicate!*
*You need to make things as easy as possible for everyone involved.*

# IT HAS TO BE 'GOOD ENOUGH'

In a program planning and project management course taught by Dr. Savithiri Ratnapalan, one thing she said will always stay with me. She said, "It has to be good enough." This in no way, shape or form implies that you should hand in crap. Instead, this means that sometimes, you have to 'get it off of your plate' and move on. This is especially true when it comes to drafts and/or getting your ideas out.

**Be aware of scope creep.** It becomes second nature to take on larger projects and additional tasks. It is important to remember that most supervisors are not trying to purposefully extend how long you stay in school. Instead, they usually recognize the importance of your work and research gaps that you can address. This likely comes from their enthusiasm for a topic and their excitement to see you excel. Once your committee agrees on certain decisions, for example, what type of analysis to conduct, get them to sign off on it and confirm that nothing further is needed. This should help to keep things moving and help prevent scope creep. A helpful hint that Dr. Monique Herbert taught me was to always return back to your original question. You will be surprised how often this helps you.

**Think feasibility.** Although it would be incredible to take on a massive, multi-stage project, discuss feasibility and timelines with your supervisor. There is nothing wrong with 'career students,' however, I am guessing you would like to graduate as quickly as possible. Anything you don't take on can be considered 'future research.'

**Set timelines and deliverables.** Once you see it all coming together, this can be an exciting time for you. Ensure you set realistic milestones and goals for yourself. To do this accurately, you must Understand the concept of 'work breakdown structure.' What am I talking about? Simply put, it is the breakdown of tasks required to complete a job.

# TASK 8

*Complete the following exercise.*

If you were to make a cup of coffee, how long would you say that it takes? Before continuing on, fill in your estimate.

Write the length of time here_____.

# TASK 9

*Okay, now complete **Table 9** on the next page. Let's look at all of the steps involved in making a cup of instant coffee.*

*In the left column, there are a series of steps involved in making a cup of coffee. They are not unreasonable; however, clearly, this is to emphasize a point.*

*In the second column, record approximately how long you think each task would take you to complete. Then, add up the time in column two. Finally, compare the total time you recorded for task 8 with the time you documented in task 9.*

## Table 9. Work Break Down Structure

| Tasks to Complete | Total Time to Accomplish |
|---|---|
| Walk to the kitchen from where you are now. | |
| Find a mug. | |
| It's dirty, wash it. | |
| Fill the pot. | |
| Boil the water. | |
| Find where you put the coffee. *(Hopefully, you did not run out, or you now have to go to the store to buy some)* | |
| Get a spoon. *(I hope it is not dirty as well...just saying)*. | |
| Unscrew the coffee jar. | |
| Take out a spoon of coffee and place it in a mug. | |
| Add the water. | |
| Stir. | |
| Did you want milk? If so, go get it. Do you have to open a new carton or jug? Did you run out and have to make a quick trip to the store? | |
| Did you want sugar? *(I hope you have or you need to run back to the store)*. | |
| Let's just stop here and forget that it has to cool a bit before you sip it or that you accidentally spilled it. | |
| **TOTAL** | |

Now that you have completed tasks 8 and 9, hopefully, you can see that sometimes things can take longer than expected. Build-in extra time. Although the example of making coffee may seem a bit silly and far-fetched, think about the implications. Ensure you constantly review your timelines and ensure that they are updated. To follow are a few different examples of helpful templates. They can remain high-level or be as detailed as you wish. Some prefer to use both.

# TASK 10

*Complete **Table 10** to the best of your ability. Realize that things will change. Review regularly.*

## Table 10. Timeline

|  | Item | Will Likely Take | Giving Self Extra Time | Start Date | Completed Date |
|---|---|---|---|---|---|
| E.g. | Ethics approval | 4 weeks | 6 weeks |  |  |
| 1. |  |  |  |  |  |
| 2. |  |  |  |  |  |
| 3. |  |  |  |  |  |
| 4. |  |  |  |  |  |
| 5. |  |  |  |  |  |
| 6. |  |  |  |  |  |
| 7. |  |  |  |  |  |
| 8. |  |  |  |  |  |
| 9. |  |  |  |  |  |
| 10. |  |  |  |  |  |

*Review the sample timeline, **Table 11.** Start to think about what your timeline will look like. Discuss this with your supervisor.*

## Table 11. Sample Timeline

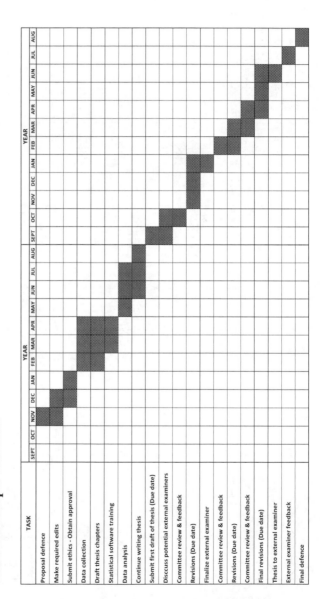

# TASK 12

*Complete **Table 12** to the best of your ability. Realize that things will change. Once again, review regularly.*

## Table 12. Timeline Template

| Task | YEAR ONE | | | | | | | | | | | | YEAR TWO | | | | | | | | | | | | YEAR THREE | | | | | | | | | | | | YEAR FOUR | | | | | | | | | | | |
|------|------|-----|-----|-----|-----|-----|-----|-----|-----|-----|-----|-----|------|-----|-----|-----|-----|-----|-----|-----|-----|-----|-----|-----|------|-----|-----|-----|-----|-----|-----|-----|-----|-----|-----|-----|------|-----|-----|-----|-----|-----|-----|-----|-----|-----|-----|-----|
| | SEPT | OCT | NOV | DEC | JAN | FEB | MAR | APR | MAY | JUN | JUL | AUG | SEPT | OCT | NOV | DEC | JAN | FEB | MAR | APR | MAY | JUN | JUL | AUG | SEPT | OCT | NOV | DEC | JAN | FEB | MAR | APR | MAY | JUN | JUL | AUG | SEPT | OCT | NOV | DEC | JAN | FEB | MAR | APR | MAY | JUN | JUL | AUG |

33

# EXPECT THE UNEXPECTED

The one thing you can count on is that the unexpected will occur. People go on vacation when you need signatures – how dare they have lives. You may experience delays with ethics approval and/or data collection. You discover analytic software glitches or problems with your data analysis. Then, right when you think you have a great proposal, some brilliant researcher on the other side of the world thought about it just a little bit earlier and steals your thunder.

Heaven forbid, but it does happen; what if your supervisor dies? Yes, this did happen to a friend of mine. Now pending on how well you got along, I guess this is one way out of the relationship.

**Stressed?** Oh, you will be. Just remember, as my partner always says, you are not saving babies. Unless you are working in that field, of course, then you are unable to use this excuse. Enjoy the process, expect delays, and communicate with your supervisor. Build-in extra time for the unexpected. You will feel great when you are ahead of schedule. There is nothing like saying "I am ahead of schedule" at one of your progress report meetings. If this is the case, pat yourself on the back.

# TASK 13

*Take a few moments and complete **Table 13** below. Other than the unexpected illness or tragedy – fingers crossed, no whammies - What are the areas where you could potentially encounter delays? You are not expected to have a complete list, but at least start thinking about it.*

**Table 13. Potential Delays**

|      | Item |
|------|------|
| E.g. | Ethics approval |
| 1.   |      |
| 2.   |      |
| 3.   |      |
| 4.   |      |
| 5.   |      |
| 6.   |      |
| 7.   |      |
| 8.   |      |
| 9.   |      |
| 10.  |      |

When you meet with your supervisor, discuss your list and see if they have any other additions.

# SELECTING EXAMINERS

You are becoming an expert in your field. Speak with your supervisor about potential examiners and have them suggest a few as well. If you can't think of anyone, consider looking through your reference list for individuals frequently cited. Once you identify someone, find out how this person has worked in the past as an external examiner. Were they fair? Look up your examiner and become familiar with their research. Work with your supervisor to agree upon a defence date and book your examiner as early as possible. You do not want their availability to be a bottleneck and slow you down.

# PROPOSAL - AKA 'THE CONVERSATION'

If your program does not require a proposal, lucky you. Feel free to skip ahead, or better yet, continue reading and be happy that this section does not apply to you.

Many students go into their proposal terrified that they have to defend their work. Don't get me wrong, you need to know your research inside and out. You need to recall why particular decisions were made. However, what I did not realize was that this is a conversation. This is the time to listen, ask questions, and explain what you have done to date. I was in absolute shock when I realized that my external thought I was trying to do too much. Examiners are not out to get you; they are there to help you, challenge you, and make sure that your research and timelines are feasible.

For those who have no idea of what to expect, here is a brief overview. You are often required to provide a written proposal and, in some cases, a short oral presentation. Length of the written proposal may vary depending on whether you are completing a master's or doctorate. For example, one might expect a master's written submission to be approximately 20 to 30 pages in length. In comparison, a doctoral proposal is more likely 30 to 40 pages. At a minimum, both will likely include the following sections:

- Title
- The Problem
- Background Information and Theoretical Frameworks
- Design and Methods
- Data Analysis
- Workplan (Timelines)

Obviously, this will differ pending your degree; however, discuss this with your supervisor or program director.

# FINAL DEFENCE – 'THE BIG HURRAH'

As per your proposal, you are often required to do an oral defence and a written dissertation. In general, the length and sections will vary depending on your thesis, department, graduate school, supervisor preference, etc. Your school likely has a template for your written component. As you publish and complete sections of your thesis, start filling in your template. Why wait until the end?

Depending on your graduate school policies, you should receive feedback from your external reviewer ahead of your defence. This will give you a general idea regarding the questions they are going to ask. Once you have this feedback, address as many of their questions or concerns in your presentation.

Before you start your oral defence, stop and take a deep breath. The best advice I received regarding my defence was to simply think of it as showcasing your work. This is your time to shine. You have the stage. You must know all of the decisions made along the way and why those decisions were made.

An excellent way to start your presentation is by providing context. A minute or two about why you pursued this area of study. For example, did you want to learn more about autism because your child has autism? Were you interested in micro-organizational behaviour because you worked in a toxic environment and became fascinated with just how miserable some people can be? Are you a clinician with a particular area of study?

The length of your written component will vary. My thesis, for example, was 263 pages in total. For a high-level summary of what my final dissertation included, see **Sample Sections from Ty's Dissertation**.

### SAMPLE SECTIONS FROM TY'S DISSERTATION

- Table of Contents
- Acknowledgements
- List of Tables, Figures, Appendices
- Introduction and Purpose
- Background and Literature Review
- Development of Conceptual Framework and Propositions
- Methods
- Analysis
- Results
- Discussion (how do your results compare with the literature?)
- Implications (theoretical and practical)
- Study Limitations
- Future Research
- Conclusions
- References
- Appendices
- Copyright Acknowledgements (as required)

As for the oral defence, there are many 'final defence questions' available online. Regardless, be prepared to address the basics:

1. Specific questions raised by the external examiner.
2. Your major or most important findings?
3. Implications of your work.
4. Things you would do differently?
5. What next? Future Collaborations?

# CELEBRATE

Take time to celebrate and appreciate all that you have accomplished. Then, spoil yourself and those around you. It is easy to get caught up in the 'rat race' and jump right back into the swing of things. But, you worked hard, reflect on this, and congratulations.

This is a monumental achievement. Think about what you have learned. Not only about your thesis, but about you, your skills, abilities, and resilience. Continue to motivate, inspire, and lead. You are graduating at an exciting time with lots to be done. Be the change agent that we all know you are.

I will leave you with 3 pieces of advice that have served me well.

1. When you question your abilities, stop and believe in them.
2. When you feel fear, stop and seek answers.
3. When you find yourself lost, stop and find purpose.

# APPENDIX ONE

## GENIUS IDEAS

*Keep track of your ideas here. If you don't have any genius ideas yet, don't feel bad. They will come to you.*

# APPENDIX TWO

## MEETING TEMPLATE A

**Attendees:**                                          **Date:**
                                                        **Time:**

**Agenda**

1.
2.
3.
4.
5.

**Action Items**          **Who is Responsible**          **Due Date:**
1.
2.
3.

**Next Meeting:**          **Date:**                      **Time:**

Printed in the United States
by Baker & Taylor Publisher Services